grac e

VISUAL EDITION

Philip Yancey

creative direction by
mark arnold

andArnold books

We would like to hear from you. Please send your comments about this book to us in care of the address below. Thank you.

ZONDERVAN

Grace

Copyright © 2003, 2010 by Philip D. Yancey and SCCT

Previously published as *What's So Amazing about Grace Visual Edition* 2003

Text based on *What's So Amazing about Grace*

Copyright © 1997 by Philip D. Yancey and SCCT

This title is also available as a Zondervan ebook. Visit www.zondervan.com/ebooks.

Requests for information should be addressed to:

Zondervan, *Grand Rapids, Michigan 49530*

ISBN 978-0-310-29319-4

Creative direction and design by Mark Arnold, andArnold Books.

Printed in the United States of America

10 11 12 13 14 /SBM/ 20 19 18 17 16 15 14 13 12 11 10 9 8 7 6 5 4 3 2 1

ZONDERVAN.com

ZONDERVAN.com/
AUTHORTRACKER
follow your favorite authors

Introduction to Visual Edition

BY PHILIP YANCEY

I MUST ADMIT, it took me a while to warm up to the idea of someone messing with my book! As I thought about it, though, I realized that people encounter grace in ways other than words. As I have written, I experienced grace first through nature, music, and romantic love, and only later found words to interpret and express what I had felt. Why not let some very skilled designers select passages from my book and interpret them visually? (Okay, I secretly hope that if you like this book you'll look up the full-text version of *What's So Amazing about Grace?* It may seem boring in contrast to this edition, but it may also fill in some gaps.)

Almost a million copies of my book have been sold, which says something about our thirst for grace. I have received thousands of letters from readers, some grateful, some desperate, some furious. One of my favorites thanks me profusely for my book *What's So Annoying About Grace?* I'm sure, from the tone of the letter, that the reader meant to write "Amazing" and typed "Annoying" by mistake. Many other letters, however, come from readers who truly do find grace annoying.

Must we forgive everyone? Shouldn't people have to pay for their mistakes? Would God forgive Saddam Hussein or Hitler? What about justice and fairness? How can you keep people from taking advantage of grace? These are some of the questions readers have tossed back at me. I imagine some readers will find this visual edition even more annoying because it presents the scandal of grace more directly, more "in your face."

I cannot claim that grace is fair. By definition, it's unfair: We get the opposite of what we deserve. I wrote my book to make a simple point, the same point a slave trader named John Newton made several centuries ago. Grace is amazing—the most amazing, perplexing, powerful force in the universe, I believe, and the only hope for our twisted, violent planet. If you catch a mere whiff of its scent, it could change your life forever.

makes

ugly

PHOTO: Rain on a windshield at night

A - maz - ing
Amazing

A - maz - ing
grace

8

grac

grac
grace

ing

g

9

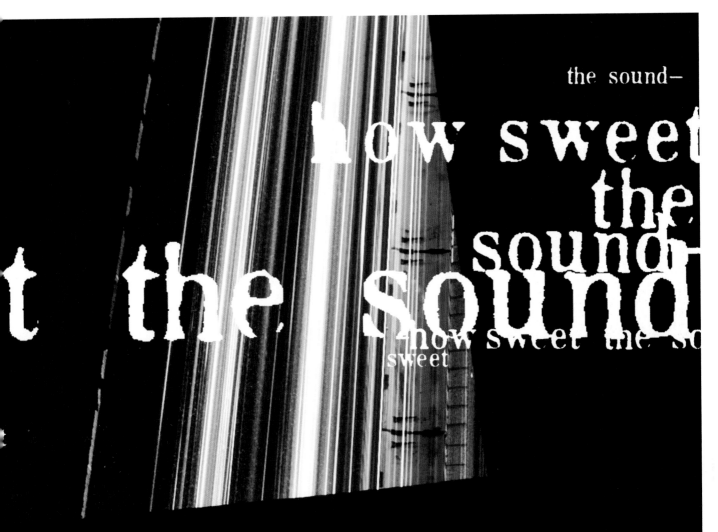

sweet

sweet – That saved a

the sound—
sweet

wretch

like me.

like me.

like me.

13

like me.
like me.
like me. like me. like me. like me.
like me. like me.
like me. like me.
like me. like me.
like me. like me.
like me. like me. like me.
like me. like me. like me.

like me.

like me.

16

"Jesus did not identify the person with his sin, but rather saw in this sin SOMETHING ALIEN, something that really did not belong to him, something that merely chained and mastered him and from which he would free him and bring him back to his real self. Jesus was able to love men because he loved them right through the layer of mud." ---HELMUT THIELICKE

SPAIN. GAILICA. Santiago Cathedral. A group of ex-drug addicts arrive at the Cathedral after fifteen days walking. On arrival they are given a letter from their parents and family; the letter is unexpected and most of them burst into prolonged crying. The group is part of Encorde 98, a charity based in Valencia who run a one-and-a-half-year program.

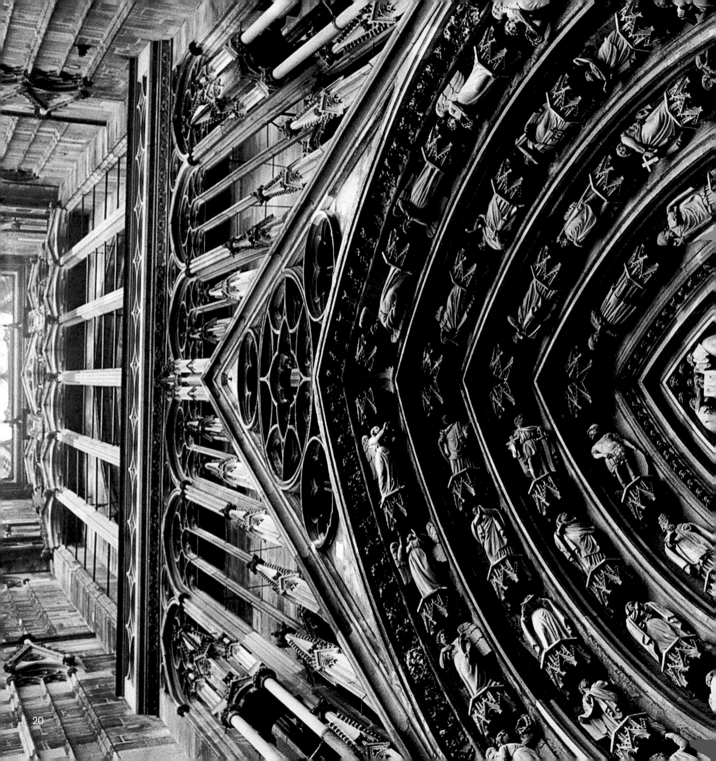

"A PROSTITUTE came to me in wretched straits, homeless, sick, unable to buy food for her two-year-old daughter. Through sobs and tears, she told me she had been renting out her daughter—two years old!—to men interested in kinky sex. She made more renting out her daughter for an hour than she could earn on her own in a night. She had to do it, she said, to support her own drug habit.

I could hardly bear hearing her sordid story. For one thing, it made me legally liable—I'm required to report cases of child abuse. I had no idea what to say to this woman. At last I asked if she had ever thought of going to a church for help. I will never forget the look of pure, naive shock that crossed her face. 'Church!' she cried. 'Why would I ever go there? I was already feeling terrible about myself. They'd just make me feel worse.'"

What struck me about my friend's story is that women much like this prostitute fled toward Jesus, not away from him. The worse a person felt about herself, the more likely she saw Jesus as a refuge. Has the church lost that gift? Evidently the down-and-out, who flocked to Jesus when he lived on earth, no longer feel welcome among his followers.

PART ONE ⇾ IN 1898

DAISY was born into a working-class Chicago family, the eighth child of ten. The father barely earned enough to feed them all, and after he took up drinking, money got much scarcer. Daisy, closing in on her hundredth birthday as I write this, shudders when she talks about those days. Her father was a "mean drunk," she says. Daisy used to cower in the corner, sobbing, as he kicked her baby brother and sister across the linoleum floor. She hated him with all her heart. One day the father declared that he wanted his wife out of the house by noon. All ten kids crowded around their mother, clinging to her skirt and crying, "No, don't go!" But their father did not back down. Holding on to her brothers and sisters for support, Daisy watched through the bay window as her mother walked down the sidewalk, shoulders adroop, a suitcase in each hand, growing smaller and smaller until finally she disappeared from view. ⊰ Some of the children eventually rejoined their mother, and some went to live with other relatives. It fell to Daisy to stay with her father. She grew up with a hard knot of bitterness inside her, a tumor of hatred over what he had done to the family. All the kids dropped out of school early in order to take jobs or join the Army, and then one by one they moved away to other towns. They got married, started families, and tried to put the past behind them. The father vanished—no one knew where and no one cared. ⊰ Many years later, to everyone's surprise, the father resurfaced. He had guttered out, he said. Drunk and cold, he had wandered into a Salvation Army rescue mission one night. To earn a meal ticket he first had to attend a worship service. When the speaker asked if anyone wanted to accept Jesus, he thought it only polite to go forward along with some of the other drunks. He was more surprised than anybody when the "sinner's prayer" actually worked. The demons inside him quieted down. He sobered up. He began studying the Bible and praying. For the first time in his life he felt loved.

and accepted. He felt clean. ⇉ And now, he told his children, he was looking them up one by one to ask for forgiveness. He couldn't defend anything that had happened. He couldn't make it right. But he was sorry, more sorry than they could possibly imagine. The children, now middle-aged and with families of their own, were initially skeptical. Some doubted his sincerity, expecting him to fall off the wagon at any moment. Others figured he would soon ask for money. Neither

happened, and in time the father won them over, all except Daisy. ⇉ Long ago Daisy had vowed never to speak to her father—"that man" she called him—again. Her father's reappearance rattled her badly, and old memories of his drunken rages came flooding back as she lay in bed at night. "He can't undo all that just by saying 'I'm sorry,'" Daisy insisted. She wanted no part of him. ⇉ The father may have given up drinking, but alcohol had damaged his liver beyond repair. He got very sick, and for the last five years of his life he lived with one of his daughters, Daisy's sister. They lived, in fact, eight houses down the street from Daisy, on the very same row house block. Keeping her vow, Daisy never once stopped in to visit her dying father, even though she passed by his house whenever she went grocery shopping or caught a bus. ⇉ Daisy did consent to let her own children visit their grandfather. Nearing the end, the father saw a little girl come to his door and step inside. "Oh, Daisy, Daisy, you've come to me at last," he cried, gathering her in his arms. The adults in the room didn't have the heart to tell him the girl was not Daisy, but her daughter Margaret. He was hallucinating grace. continued

on page 58

avoiders
o.f conta
gion

We ourselves can be agents of God's holiness,

for God now dwells within us.

In the midst of an unclean world we can stride,

as Jesus did, seeking ways to be a source of holiness.

The sick and the maimed

are not hot spots of

contamination but

potential reservoirs of God's mercy.

conveyers of grace conveyers of grace conveyers of grace conveyers of grace conveyers of grace conveyers of grace conveyers of grace conveyers of grace conveyers of grace conveyers of grace conveyers of grace conveyers of grace

25

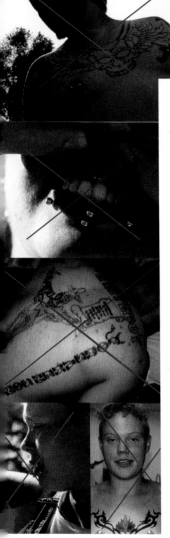

✕ A U.S. DELEGATE to the Baptist World Alliance Congress in Berlin in 1934 sent back this report of what he found under Hitler's regime: "It was a great relief to be in a country where salacious sex literature cannot be sold; where putrid motion pictures and gangster films cannot be shown. The new Germany has burned great masses of corrupting books and magazines along with its bonfires of Jewish and communistic libraries." The same delegate defended Hitler as a leader who did not smoke or drink, who wanted women to dress modestly, and who opposed pornography. ✕ ✕ ✕ ✕ ✕ ✕ It is all too easy to point fingers at German Christians of the 1930s, southern fundamentalists in the 1960s, or South African Calvinists of the 1970s. What sobers me is that contemporary Christians may someday be judged as harshly. What trivialities do we obsess over, and what weighty matters of the law—justice, mercy, faithfulness—might we be missing? DOES GOD CARE MORE about nose rings or about urban decay? Grunge music or world hunger? Worship styles or a culture of violence? ✕ ✕ ✕ Author Tony Campolo, who makes a regular circuit as a chapel speaker on Christian college campuses, for a time used this provocation to make a point. "The United Nations reports that over ten thousand people starve to death each day, and most of you don't give a shit. However, what is even more tragic is that most of you are more concerned about the fact that I just said a bad word than you are about the fact that ten thousand people are going to die today." The responses proved his point: in nearly every case Tony got a letter from the chaplain or president of the college protesting his foul language. The letters never mentioned world hunger.

Famine in Somalia.

Not long ago I received in the mail a postcard from a friend that had on it only six words, "I am the one Jesus loves." I smiled when I saw the return address, for my strange friend excels at these pious slogans. When I called him, though, he told me the slogan came from the author and speaker Brennan Manning. At a seminar, Manning referred to Jesus' closest friend on earth, the disciple named John, identified in the Gospels as "the one Jesus loved." Manning said, "If John were to be asked, 'What is your primary identity in life?' he would not reply, 'I am a disciple, an apostle, an evangelist, an author of one of the four Gospels,' but rather, 'I am the one Jesus loves.'"

What would it mean, I ask myself, if I too came to the place where I saw my primary identity in life as "the one Jesus loves"? How differently would I view myself at the end of the day?

Sociologists have a theory of the looking-glass self: you become what the most important person in your life (wife, father, boss, etc.) thinks you are. How would my life change if I truly believed the Bible's astounding words about God's love for me, if I looked in the mirror and saw what God sees?

Brennan Manning tells the story of an Irish priest who, on a walking tour of a rural parish, sees an old peasant kneeling by the side of the road, praying. Impressed, the priest says to the man, "You must be very close to God." The peasant looks up from his prayers, thinks a moment, and then smiles, "Yes, he's very fond of me."

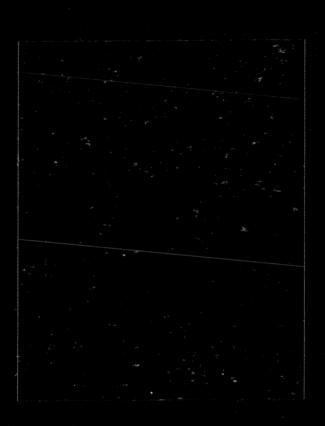

The one Jesus loves.

God dispenses

not wages.

gifts,

Grace means there is nothing we can do to make God love us more—no amount of **SPIRITUAL CALISTHENICS** and **RENUNCIATIONS**, no amount of **KNOWLEDGE** gained from **SEMINARS** and **DIVINITY SCHOOLS**, no amount of **CRUSADING** on behalf of **RIGHTEOUS CAUSES**.

And grace means there is nothing we can do to make God love us less—no amount of **RACISM** or **PRIDE** or **POR-NOGRAPHY** or **ADULTERY** or even **MURDER.**

WE HAVE MANY VIVID DEMONSTRATIONS OF THE LAW OF UNFORGIVENESS. IN SHAKESPEARE'S AND SOPHOCLES' HISTORICAL TRAGEDIES, BODIES LITTER THE STAGE. *Macbeth, Richard III, Titus Andronicus,* AND *Elektra* MUST KILL AND KILL AND KILL UNTIL THEY HAVE THEIR REVENGE, THEN LIVE IN FEAR LEST SOME ENEMIES HAVE SURVIVED TO SEEK COUNTER REVENGE.

FRANCIS FORD COPPOLA'S *Godfather* TRILOGY AND CLINT EASTWOOD'S *Unforgiven* ILLUSTRATE THE SAME LAW. WE SEE THE LAW AT WORK IN IRA TERRORISTS WHO BLOW UP SHOPPERS IN DOWN-TOWN LONDON IN PART BECAUSE OF ATROCITIES COMMITTED BACK IN 1649—WHICH IN TURN WERE ORDERED BY OLIVER CROMWELL TO AVENGE A MASSACRE IN 1641.

like me.

The Bible's many fierce passages on sin appear in a new light once I understand God's desire to press me toward repentance, the doorway to grace. Jesus told Nicodemus, "For God did not send his Son into the world to condemn the world, but to save the world through him." In other words, he awakens guilt for my own benefit. God seeks not to crush me but to liberate me. "It is the saints who have a sense of sin," as Father Danielou says; "The sense of sin is the measure of a soul's awareness of God."

IN CHURCH THE OTHER SUNDAY I was intent on a small child who was turning around smiling at everyone. He wasn't gurgling, spitting, humming, kicking, tearing the hymnals, or rummaging through his mother's handbag. He was just smiling. Finally, his mother jerked him about and in a stage whisper that could be heard in a little theatre off Broadway said, "Stop that grinning! You're in church!" With that, she gave him a belt and as the tears rolled down his cheeks added, "That's better," and returned to her prayers.... ■ ■ Suddenly I was angry. It occurred to me the entire world is in tears, and if you're not, then you'd better get with it. I wanted to grab this child with the tear-stained face close to me and tell him about MY GOD. THE HAPPY GOD. THE SMILING GOD. The God who had to have a sense of humor to have created the likes of us... By tradition, one wears faith with the solemnity of a mourner, the gravity of a mask of tragedy, and the dedication of a Rotary badge. ■ ■ ■ What a fool, I thought. Here was a woman sitting next to the only light left in our civilization— the only hope, our only miracle—our only promise of infinity. If he couldn't smile in church, where was there left to go? ■ ■ ■

— ERMA BOMBECK

"Jesus gained the power to love because he saw through the filth and crust of degeneration,

because his eye caught THE DIVINE ORIGINAL which is hidden in every way—

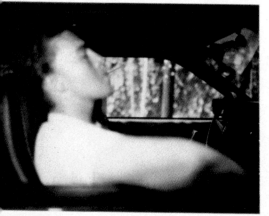

in every man! . . . First and foremost he gives us new eyes." ---HELMUT THIELICKE

42

Will Campbell grew up on a hardscrabble farm in Mississippi. Bookish, never really fitting in with his rural surroundings, he worked hard at his studies and eventually made his way to Yale Divinity School. After graduation he returned south to preach and was named director of religious life at the University of Mississippi. This was the early 1960s, when proper Mississippians circled the wagons against assaults from civil rights activists, and when students and administrators learned of Campbell's liberal views on integration, his stint at the school abruptly ended.

CAMPBELL SOON FOUND HIMSELF IN THE THICK OF THE BATTLE, leading voter registration drives and supervising the idealistic young Northerners who migrated south to join the civil rights crusade. Among them was a Harvard Divinity School student named Jonathan Daniels, who had responded to Dr. King's call for supporters to descend on Selma. Most of the volunteers went home after the big march, but Jonathan Daniels stayed, and Will Campbell befriended him.

CAMPBELL'S THEOLOGY WAS UNDERGOING SOME TESTING IN THOSE DAYS. MUCH OF THE OPPOSITION TO HIS WORK CAME FROM "GOOD CHRISTIANS" WHO REFUSED TO LET PEOPLE OF OTHER RACES INTO THEIR CHURCHES AND WHO RESENTED ANYONE TAMPERING WITH LAWS FAVORING WHITE PEOPLE. CAMPBELL FOUND ALLIES MORE EASILY AMONG AGNOSTICS, SOCIALISTS, AND A FEW DEVOUT NORTHERNERS.

"In ten words or less, what's the Christian message?" one agnostic had challenged him. The interlocutor was P.D. East, a renegade newspaper editor who viewed Christians as the enemy and could not understand Will's stubborn commitment to religious faith.

We were going someplace, or coming back from someplace when he said, 'Let me have it. Ten words.' I said, "We're all bastards but God loves us anyway." He didn't comment on what he thought about the summary except to say, after he counted the number of words on his fingers, 'I gave you a ten-word limit. If you want to try again you have two words left.' I didn't try again but he often reminded me of what I had said that day.

THE DEFINITION STUNG P.D. EAST WHO, UNBEKNOWN TO CAMPBELL, WAS INDEED ILLEGITIMATE AND HAD BEEN CALLED "BASTARD" ALL HIS LIFE. CAMPBELL HAD CHOSEN THE WORD NOT MERELY FOR SHOCK EFFECT BUT ALSO FOR THEOLOGICAL ACCURACY: SPIRITUALLY WE ARE ILLEGITIMATE CHILDREN, INVITED DESPITE OUR PATERNITY TO JOIN GOD'S FAMILY. THE MORE CAMPBELL THOUGHT ABOUT HIS IMPROMPTU DEFINITION OF THE GOSPEL, THE MORE HE LIKED IT.

P.D. East put that definition to a ruthless test, however, on the darkest day of Campbell's life, a day when an Alabama deputy sheriff named Thomas Coleman gunned down Campbell's twenty-six-year-old friend. Jonathan Daniels had been arrested for picketing white stores. On his release from jail he approached a grocery store to make a phone call to arrange a ride when Coleman appeared with a shotgun and emptied it in his stomach. The pellets hit one other person, a black teenager, in the back, critically injuring him.

Campbell's book Brother to a Dragonfly records the conversation with P.D. East on that night, which led to what Campbell looks back on as "the most enlightening theological lesson I ever had in my life." P.D. East stayed on the offensive, even at this moment of grief:

(con't)

"YEA, BROTHER. LET'S SEE IF YOUR DEFINITION OF THE FAITH CAN STAND THE TEST." My calls had been to the Department of Justice, to the American Civil Liberties Union, and to a lawyer friend in Nashville. I had talked of the death of my friend as being a travesty of justice, as a complete breakdown of law and order, as a violation of Federal and State law. I HAD USED WORDS LIKE REDNECK, BACKWOODS, WOOL HAT, CRACKER, KLUXER, IGNORAMUS AND MANY OTHERS. I HAD STUDIED SOCIOLOGY, PSYCHOLOGY, AND SOCIAL ETHICS AND WAS SPEAKING AND THINKING IN THOSE CONCEPTS. I HAD ALSO STUDIED NEW TESTAMENT THEOLOGY.

P.D. stalked me like a tiger. "Come on, Brother. Let's talk about your definition." At one point Joe (Will's brother) turned on him, "Lay off, P.D. Can't you see when somebody is upset?" But P.D. waved him off, loving me too much to leave me alone.

"Was Jonathan a bastard?" P.D. asked first.

Campbell replied that though he was one of the most gentle guys he'd ever known, it's true that everyone is a sinner. In those terms, yes, he was a "bastard."

"All right. Is Thomas Coleman a bastard?"

That question, Campbell found much easier to answer. You bet the murderer was a bastard.

Then P.D. pulled his chair close, placed his bony hand on Campbell's knee, and looked directly into his red-streaked eyes. "Which one of these two bastards do you think God loves the most?" The question hit home, like an arrow to the heart.

SUDDENLY everything became clear. EVERYthing. It was
a revelation. The glow of the malt which we were well into
by then seemed to illuminate and intensify it. I walked
across the room and opened the blind, staring directly into
the glare of the streetlight. And I began to whimper. But
the crying was interspersed with laughter. It was a strange
experience. I remember trying to sort out the sadness and the
joy. Just what I was crying for and what I was laughing
for. Then this too became clear. I was laughing at myself, at twenty years of a ministry
which had become, without my realizing it, a ministry
of liberal sophistication. . . .

I agreed that the notion that a man could go to a store where
a group of unarmed human beings are drinking soda pop and
eating moon pies, fire a shotgun blast at one of them, tearing
his lungs and heart and bowels from his body, turn on another
and send lead pellets ripping through his flesh and bones, and
that God would

SET HIM FREE is almost more than I could stand.
But unless that is precisely the case then there
is no Gospel, there is no Good News. Unless that is
the truth we have only bad news; we are back with
law alone.

WHAT WILL CAMPBELL LEARNED THAT NIGHT
WAS A NEW INSIGHT INTO GRACE. THE
FREE OFFER OF GRACE EXTENDS NOT JUST
TO THE UNDESERVING BUT TO THOSE WHO
IN FACT DESERVE THE OPPOSITE: TO KU
KLUX KLANNERS AS WELL AS CIVIL RIGHTS
MARCHERS, TO P.D. EAST AS WELL AS WILL
CAMPBELL, TO THOMAS COLEMAN AS WELL AS
JONATHAN DANIELS.

This message lodged so deep inside Will Campbell
that he underwent a kind of earthquake of grace. He
resigned his position with the National Council of
Churches and became what he wryly calls "an apostle
to the rednecks." He bought a farm in Tennessee, and
today is as likely to spend his time among Klansmen
and racists as among racial minorities and white
liberals. A LOT OF PEOPLE, HE DECIDED, WERE
VOLUNTEERING TO HELP MINORITIES; HE KNEW OF
NO ONE MINISTERING TO THE THOMAS COLEMANS
OF THE WORLD.

like me.

like me.

like me.

like me.

48

like me.

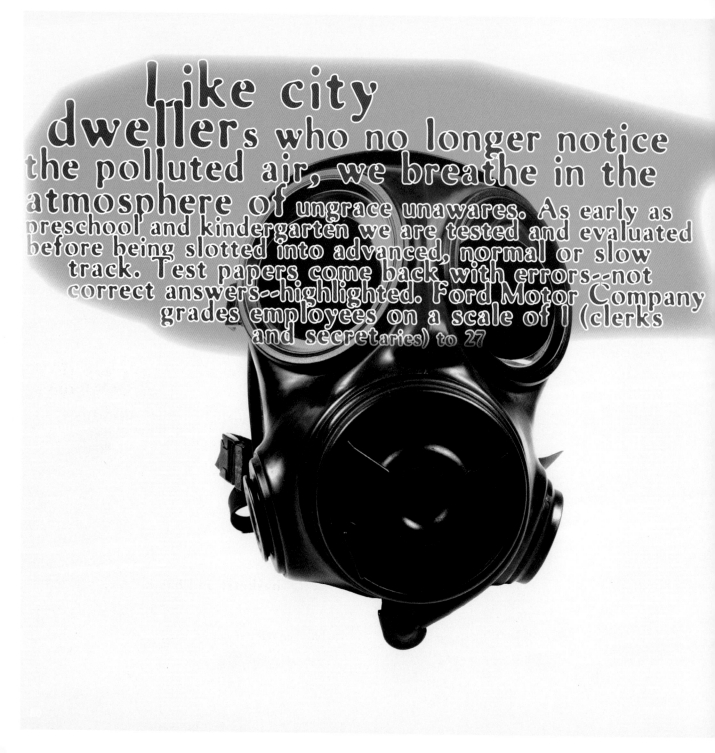

Like city dwellers who no longer notice the polluted air, we breathe in the atmosphere of ungrace unawares. As early as preschool and kindergarten we are tested and evaluated before being slotted into advanced, normal or slow track. Test papers come back with errors--not correct answers--highlighted. Ford Motor Company grades employees on a scale of 1 (clerks and secretaries) to 27

(chairman
of the board). You must be
at least Grade 9 to qualify for a parking
space: Grade 13 brings with it such perks as a
window, plants and an intercom system: Grade 16
Offices come equipped with private bathrooms.
Justice departments and mortgage companies
cannnot operate by grace.

A sports franchise
rewards those who
complete

passes,
throw strikes, or make

baskets, and has no
place for those who fail. Fortune Magazine

annually lists the five hundred richest: no one knows
the
names of the five

hundred

poorest.

Grace is

fair.

not

the

murdered   *OR*

Which one does God love the most?

the

murderer

It is easy to love the people far away. It is not always easy to love those close to us. It is easier to give a cup of rice to relieve hunger than to relieve the loneliness and pain of someone unloved in our own home. Bring love into your home for this is where our love for each other must start. Each one of them is Jesus in disguise. —MOTHER TERESA

PART TWO ⋨ ALL
HER LIFE Daisy determined to be unlike her father, and indeed she never touched a drop of alcohol. Yet she ruled her own family with a milder form of the tyranny she had grown up under. She would lie on a couch with a rubber ice pack on her head and scream at the kids to "Shut up!" "Why did I ever have you stupid kids anyway?" she would yell. "You've ruined my life!" The Great Depression had hit, and each child was one more mouth to feed. She had six in all, rearing them in the two-bedroom row house she lives in to this day. In such close quarters, they seemed always underfoot. Some nights she gave them all whippings just to make a point: she knew they'd done wrong even if she hadn't caught them. ⇉ Hard as steel, Daisy never apologized and never forgave. Her daughter Margaret remembers as a child coming in tears to apologize for something she'd done. Daisy responded with a parental Catch-22: "You can't possibly be sorry! If you were really sorry, you wouldn't have done it in the first place." ⇉ I have heard many such stories of ungrace from Margaret, whom I know well. All her life she determined to be different from her mother, Daisy. But Margaret's life had its own tragedies, some large and some small, and as her four children entered their teenage years she felt she was losing control of them. She too wanted to lie on the couch with an ice pack and scream, "Shut up!" She too wanted to whip them just to make a point or maybe to release some of the tension coiled inside her. Her son Michael, who turned sixteen in the 1960s, especially got under her skin. He listened to rock and roll

wore "granny glasses," let his hair grow long. Margaret kicked him out of the house when she caught him smoking pot, and he moved into a hippie commune. ⇄ She continued to threaten and scold him. She reported him to a judge. She wrote him out of her will. She tried everything she could think of, and nothing got through to Michael. The words she flung up against him fell back, useless, until finally one day in a fit of anger she said, "I never want to see you again as long as I live." That was twenty-six years ago and she has not seen him since. ⇄ Michael is also my close friend. Several times during those twenty-six years I have attempted some sort of reconciliation between the two, and each time I confront again the terrible power of ungrace. When I asked Margaret if she regretted anything she had said to her son, if she'd like to take anything back, she turned on me in a flash of hot rage as if I were Michael himself, "I don't know why God didn't take him long ago, for all the things he's done!" she said, with a wild, scary look in her eye. Her brazen fury caught me off guard. I stared at her for a minute: her hands clenched, her face florid, tiny muscles twitching around her eyes. ⇄ "Do you mean you wish your own son was dead?" I asked at last. She never answered. continued on page 88

J 3:16

For God loved the world so much that he gave his only Son, so that everyone who believes in him may not die but have eternal life.

QANA, LEBANON

&17

For God did not send his Son into the world to be its judge, but to be its savior.

God in heaven

holds

each person by
a string.
When you sin, you cut

the string.
                    Then God ties
it up again,

making a
    knot—
and thereby bringing
you
a little closer to him.

Again

and

again

your sins cut the

string—
            and with each
further knot God

keeps drawing you

closer and
closer

and closer
closer

63

"FAGGOTS GO HOME!"

the leader screamed into a microphone, and the others took up the chant:

Faggots go home!

Faggots go home!

Faggots go home! # SHAME-ON-YOU-FOR-WHAT-YOU-DO!

Between chants the leader delivered brimstone SERMONETTES about God reserving the hottest fires in hell for sodomites and other perverts.

"AIDS, AIDS, IT'S COMIN' YOUR WAY!"
"AIDS, AIDS, IT'S COMIN' YOUR WAY!"
"AIDS, AIDS, IT'S COMIN' YOUR WAY!"

We had just seen a sad procession of several hundred persons with AIDS: many in wheelchairs, with the gaunt bodies of concentration camp survivors. Listening to the chant, I could not fathom how anyone could wish that fate on another human being.

For their part, the gay marchers had a mixed response to the Christians. More than a thousand marched under the banner of the Metropolitan Community Church, a denomination that professes a mostly evangelical theology except for its stance on homosexuality. This last group had a poignant reply to the beleaguered Christian protesters: they drew even, turned to face them, and sang,

"Jesus loves us, this we know, for the Bible tells us so."

The abrupt ironies in that scene of confrontation struck me. On the one side were "Christians" defending pure doctrine. On the other side were "sinners," many of whom openly admit to homosexual practice. Yet the more orthodox group spewed out hate and the other group sang of Jesus' love.

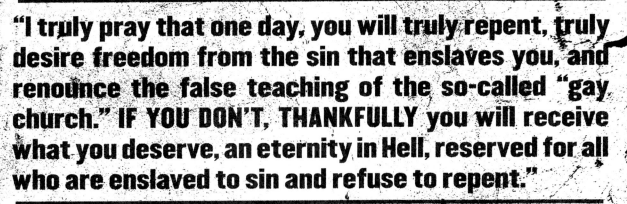

"We get such hatred and rejection FROM THE CHURCH that there's no reason to bother with church at all unless you really do believe the gospel is true."

"I truly pray that one day, you will truly repent, truly desire freedom from the sin that enslaves you, and renounce the false teaching of the so-called "gay church." IF YOU DON'T, THANKFULLY you will receive what you deserve, an eternity in Hell, reserved for all who are enslaved to sin and refuse to repent."

"WE UNDERSTAND WHERE YOU STAND, AND KNOW THAT YOU DO NOT AGREE WITH US. BUT YOU STILL SHOW THE LOVE OF JESUS, AND WE'RE DRAWN TO THAT."

To many AIDS patients in Grand Rapids, the word Christian now carries a very different connotation than it did a few years ago. Dobson's experience has proved that Christians can have firm views about ethical behavior and still demonstrate love. "I would feel proud, if I die and someone stands up at my funeral and says nothing but,

'ED DOBSON LOVED HOMOSEXUALS.'

"AS A GAY MAN, I'VE FOUND IT'S EASIER FOR ME TO GET SEX ON THE STREETS THAN TO GET A HUG IN CHURCH."

"Well," the mother answered *in a sweet, quavery voice,* "he *may be an abomination, but he's still our pride and joy."*

IN SOME WAYS WE ARE ALL ABOMINATIONS TO GOD—ALL HAVE SINNED...AND YET SOMEHOW,***AGAINST ALL REASON, GOD LOVES US ANYHOW.*****WE ARE STILL GOD'S PRIDE AND JOY.*************

SUCH PROFOUND DIFFERENCES, in whatever arena, form a kind of crucible of grace. Some must grapple with how to treat fundamentalists who wounded them in the past. Some take on the task of reconciling with rednecks and Kluxers. Still others contend with the arrogance and close-mindedness of "politically correct" liberals. Whites must deal with how they differ from African-Americans, and vice versa. Inner-city blacks must also sort out complicated relationships with Jews and Koreans.

An issue like homosexuality presents a special case because the difference centers on a moral, not a cross-cultural, issue. For most of history the church has overwhelmingly viewed homosexual behavior as a serious sin. Then the question becomes, "How do we treat sinners?"

I think of the changes that have occurred within the evangelical church in my lifetime over the issue of divorce, an issue on which Jesus is absolutely clear. Yet today a divorced person is not shunned, banned from churches, spit upon, screamed at. Even those who consider divorce a sin have come to accept the sinners and treat them with civility and even love. *OTHER SINS ON WHICH THE BIBLE IS ALSO CLEAR—GREED, FOR EXAMPLE—SEEM TO POSE NO BARRIER AT ALL.* We have learned to accept the person without approving of the behavior.

My study of Jesus' life convinces me that **WHATEVER BARRIERS WE MUST OVERCOME IN TREATING "DIFFERENT" PEOPLE CANNOT COMPARE TO WHAT A HOLY GOD** *— who dwelled in the Most Holy Place, and whose presence caused fire and smoke to belch from mountaintops, bringing death to* any unclean person *who wandered near — overcame when he descended to join us on planet Earth.*

Bud Welch lost his twenty-three-year-old daughter, Julie Marie, in that Oklahoma City bombing at the hands of Timothy McVeigh. He says he went through a period of rage when he wanted Timothy dead. "I wanted him to fry," he says. "I'd have killed him myself if I'd had the chance." But there was a moment when he remembered the words of his daughter, who had been a courageous advocate for reconciliation. She used to say, "Execution teaches hatred." It wasn't long before Bud decided to interrupt that cycle of hatred and violence and arranged a visit with McVeigh's dad and family. As they met, Bud says he grew to love them dearly and to this day says he has "never felt closer to God" than amid that union. He decided to travel around the country speaking about reconciliation and against the death penalty, which teaches that some people are beyond redemption, and pleading for the life of Timothy McVeigh. He began to look in the eyes of Timothy McVeigh, the murderer, and see the image of God. He longed for him to experience love, grace, and forgiveness. —SHANE CLAIBORNE

like me.

69

News about the Nickel Mines school massacre in the heart of Amish country faded quickly in the U.S., but not worldwide. International readers were fascinated by a group who eschewed modern dress and conveniences and who responded in such an un-American fashion to an act of violence. Indeed, 2,400 articles in the world press featured the theme of forgiveness.

More than half of those who attended the murderer's funeral were Amish. "We sin, too," they said, embracing the widow of the man who killed their children. "Didn't Jesus tell us to forgive others as God has forgiven us?"

1

I forgive you.

②

I'm sorry,

ONE OF THE GREATEST CHALLENGES
of the spiritual life is to
receive God's forgiveness. There is something
in us humans that keeps us clinging to our
sins and prevents us from letting God erase
our past
and offer us a completely new beginning.
Sometimes it even seems as though I want
to prove to God my darkness is too great to
overcome. While God wants to restore me to
the full dignity of

SONSHIP,

I keep insisting that I will settle for being a
hired
SERVANT.

BUT
do I truly want to be restored to the full
responsibility of the son
?

Do I truly want to be so totally
forgiven that a completely
new way of living becomes possible
?

Do I want to break away from my
deep-rooted rebellion against God
and surrender myself so absolutely
to God's love that a new person can
emerge
?

As a hired servant,
I can still keep my distance, still revolt,
reject, strike, run away, or
complain about my pay.
As the beloved son, I have to claim my full
dignity and begin preparing myself to
become the father.

—Henri Nouwen, THE RETURN OF THE
PRODIGAL SON

The opposite of sin is grace, not virtue.

is a direct product of ungrace: hold up the ideal of beautiful, skinny models, and teenage girls will starve themselves to death in an attempt to reach that ideal. All this takes place in the United States, a supposedly egalitarian society. Other societies have refined the art of ungrace through rigid social systems based on class, race, or caste. South Africa used to assign every citizen to one of four categories: white, black, colored, and Asian (when Japanese investors objected, the government invented a new category, "honorary white people"). India's caste system was so labyrinthine that in the 1930s the British discovered a new caste they had not encountered in three centuries of presence there: assigned the role of washing clothes for the Untouchables, these poor creatures believed they would contaminate higher castes by sight, so they emerged only at night and avoided all contact with other people.

If everyone followed the "eye for an eye" principle of justice, observed Gandhi, eventually the whole world would **g o** blind.

I once read that proportionally the surface of the earth is smoother than a billiard ball ○ The heights of Mount Everest and the troughs of the Pacific Ocean are very impressive to those of us who live on this planet ○ ○ ○ But from the view of Andromeda, or even Mars, those differences matter not at all ○ That is how I see the petty behavioral differences between one Christian group and another ○ Compared to a holy and perfect God, the loftiest Everest of rules amounts to a molehill ○ ○ ○ You cannot earn God's acceptance by climbing; you must receive it as a gift ○

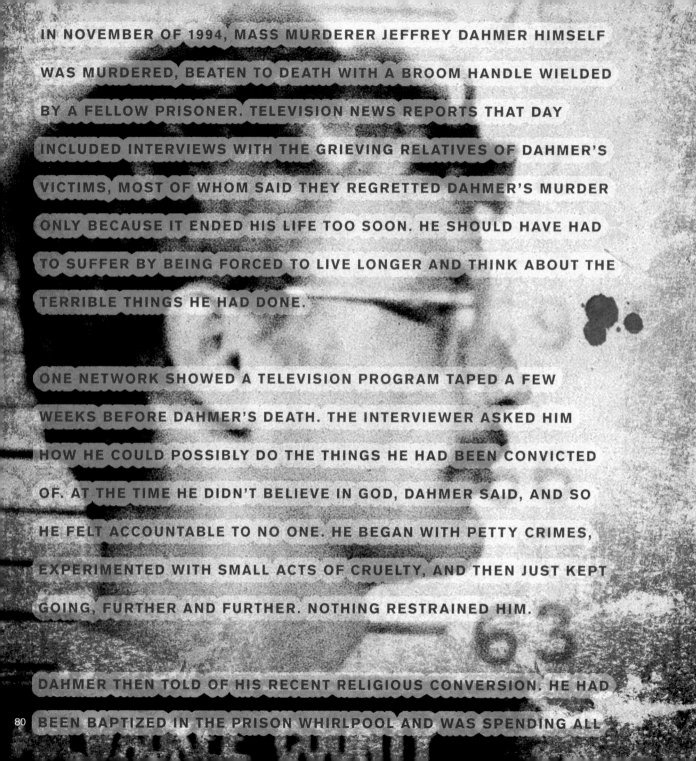

IN NOVEMBER OF 1994, MASS MURDERER JEFFREY DAHMER HIMSELF

WAS MURDERED, BEATEN TO DEATH WITH A BROOM HANDLE WIELDED

BY A FELLOW PRISONER. TELEVISION NEWS REPORTS THAT DAY

INCLUDED INTERVIEWS WITH THE GRIEVING RELATIVES OF DAHMER'S

VICTIMS, MOST OF WHOM SAID THEY REGRETTED DAHMER'S MURDER

ONLY BECAUSE IT ENDED HIS LIFE TOO SOON. HE SHOULD HAVE HAD

TO SUFFER BY BEING FORCED TO LIVE LONGER AND THINK ABOUT THE

TERRIBLE THINGS HE HAD DONE.

ONE NETWORK SHOWED A TELEVISION PROGRAM TAPED A FEW

WEEKS BEFORE DAHMER'S DEATH. THE INTERVIEWER ASKED HIM

HOW HE COULD POSSIBLY DO THE THINGS HE HAD BEEN CONVICTED

OF. AT THE TIME HE DIDN'T BELIEVE IN GOD, DAHMER SAID, AND SO

HE FELT ACCOUNTABLE TO NO ONE. HE BEGAN WITH PETTY CRIMES,

EXPERIMENTED WITH SMALL ACTS OF CRUELTY, AND THEN JUST KEPT

GOING, FURTHER AND FURTHER. NOTHING RESTRAINED HIM.

DAHMER THEN TOLD OF HIS RECENT RELIGIOUS CONVERSION. HE HAD

BEEN BAPTIZED IN THE PRISON WHIRLPOOL AND WAS SPENDING ALL

HIS TIME READING RELIGIOUS MATERIAL GIVEN TO HIM BY A LOCAL MINISTER. THE CAMERA SWITCHED TO AN INTERVIEW WITH THE PRISON CHAPLAIN, WHO AFFIRMED THAT DAHMER HAD INDEED REPENTED AND WAS NOW ONE OF HIS MOST FAITHFUL WORSHIPERS.

OUR DISCUSSION TENDED TO DIVIDE BETWEEN THOSE WHO WATCHED ONLY THE NEWS PROGRAMS ON DAHMER'S DEATH AND THOSE WHO HAD WATCHED THE INTERVIEW WITH DAHMER. THE FORMER GROUP SAW DAHMER AS A MONSTER, AND ANY REPORTS OF A JAILHOUSE CONVERSION THEY DISMISSED OUT-OF-HAND. THE RELATIVES' ANGUISHED FACES HAD MADE A DEEP IMPRESSION. ONE PERSON SAID CANDIDLY, "CRIMES THAT BAD CAN NEVER BE FORGIVEN. HE COULDN'T BE SINCERE."

THOSE WHO HAD SEEN THE INTERVIEW WITH DAHMER WERE NOT SO SURE. THEY AGREED HIS CRIMES WERE HEINOUS BEYOND BELIEF. YET HE HAD SEEMED CONTRITE, EVEN HUMBLE. THE CONVERSATION TURNED TO THE QUESTION, "IS ANYONE EVER BEYOND FORGIVENESS?" NO ONE LEFT THE EVENING FEELING ENTIRELY COMFORTABLE WITH THE ANSWERS. 81

In one of his last acts before death, **JESUS FORGAVE** a thief dangling on a cross, knowing full well the thief had converted out of plain fear. That thief would never study the Bible, never attend synagogue or church, and never make amends to all those he had wronged.

HE SIMPly said "Jesus, remember me," and Jesus promised, "Today you will be with me in paradise." It was another shocking reminder that grace does not depend on what we have done for God but rather what God has done for us.

Ask people what they must do to get to heaven and most reply, *"Be good."*

Jesus' stories contradict that answer. All we must do is cry,

HEL

P!

GOD WELCOMES HOME ANYone who will have him.

like me.

like me.

like me.

85

like me.

like me.

87

PART THREE > MICHAEL

EMERGED FROM the sixties mellower, his mind dulled by LSD. He moved to Hawaii, lived with a woman, left her, tried another, left her, and then got married. "Sue is the real thing," he told me when I visited him once. "This one will last." ◁ It did not last. I remember a phone conversation with Michael, interrupted by the annoying technological feature known as "call waiting." ⇉ The line clicked and Michael said, "Excuse me a second," then left me holding a silent phone receiver for at least four minutes. He apologized when he came back on. His mood had darkened. "It was Sue," he said. "We're settling some of the last financial issues of the divorce." ⇉ "I didn't know you still had contact with Sue," I said, making conversation. ⇉ "I don't!" he cut in, using almost the same tone I had heard from his mother, Margaret. "I hope I never see her again as long as I live!" ⇄ We both stayed silent for a long time. We had just been talking about Margaret, and although I said nothing it seemed to me that Michael had recognized in his own voice the tone of his mother, which was actually the tone of her mother, tracing all the way back to what happened in a Chicago row house nearly a century ago. ⇄ Like a spiritual defect encoded in the family DNA, ungrace gets passed on in an unbroken chain. ⇄

Ungrace does its work quietly and lethally, like a poisonous, undetectable gas. A father dies unforgiven. A mother who once carried a child in her own body does not speak to that child for half its life. The toxin steals on, from generation to generation. ⇄ Margaret is a devout Christian who studies the Bible every day, and once I spoke to her about the parable of the Prodigal Son. "What do you do with that parable?" I asked. "Do you hear its message of forgiveness?" ⇄ She had obviously thought about the matter, for without hesitation she replied that the parable appears in Luke 15 as a third in a series of three: lost coin, lost sheep, lost son. She said the whole point of the Prodigal Son is to demonstrate how human beings differ from inanimate objects (coins) and from animals (sheep). "People have free will," she said. "They have to be morally responsible. That boy had to come crawling back on his knees. He had to repent. That was Jesus' point."

continued on page 138

like me.

ONE WHO HAS BEEN TOUCHED BY GRACE WILL NO LONGER LOOK

ON THOSE WHO STRAY AS "THOSE EVIL PEOPLE" OR

"THOSE POOR PEOPLE WHO NEED OUR HELP."

NOR MUST WE SEARCH FOR SIGNS OF "LOVEWORTHINESS."

GRACE TEACHES US THAT GOD LOVES

BECAUSE OF WHO GOD IS, NOT BECAUSE OF WHO WE ARE.

IN HIS AUTOBIOGRAPHY, THE GERMAN PHILOSOPHER
FRIEDRICH NIETZSCHE TOLD OF HIS ABILITY TO
"SMELL"
THE INMOST PARTS OF EVERY SOUL, ESPECIALLY
THE "ABUNDANT HIDDEN DIRT AT THE BOTTOM
OF MANY A CHARACTER." NIETZSCHE WAS
A MASTER OF UNGRACE. WE ARE CALLED TO DO THE
OPPOSITE, TO SMELL
THE RESIDUE OF HIDDEN
WORTH

93

Can God forgive something as awful as
what I'm about to do?

...ible, warns the biblical write Jude, to "change the grace of our God into a license for immorality." At first a devious idea form... *It's something I want. Yeah, I know, it's wrong. But why don't I just go ahead anyway? I can always get forgiveness later.* Diet... ...e phrase "cheap grace" as a way of summarizing grace abuse. His book *The Cost of Discipleship* highlights the many ... ...s commanding Christians to attain holiness. Every call to conversion, he insisted, includes a call to discipleship, to Christli...

7 X 70 X X

It was altogether in character for the apostle Peter to pursue some mathematical formula of grace. "How many times shall I forgive my brother when he sins against me?" he asked Jesus. "Up to 7 times?" Peter was erring on the side of magnanimity, for the rabbis in his day had suggested 3 as the maximum number of times one might be expected to forgive.

"Not 7 times, but 77 times," replied Jesus in a flash.

Peter's question prompted another one of Jesus' stories, about a servant who somehow piles up a debt of several million dollars. The fact that realistically no servant could accumulate a debt so huge underscores Jesus' point: confiscating the man's family, children, and all his property would not make a dent in repaying the debt. It is unforgivable. Nevertheless the king, touched with pity, abruptly cancels the debt and lets the servant off scot-free.

The more I reflect on Jesus' parables, the more tempted I am to use the word "atrocious" to describe the mathematics of the gospel. I believe Jesus gave us these stories about grace in order to call us to step completely outside our tit-for-tat world of ungrace and enter in to God's realm of infinite grace.

95

In the movie _The Last Emperor_, the young child anointed as the last emperor of China lives a magical life of luxury with a thousand eunuch servants at his command. "What happens when you do wrong?" his brother asks." When I do wrong, someone else is punished," the boy emperor replies. To demonstrate, he breaks a jar, and one of the servants is beaten.

Jesus reversed that ancient pattern: when the servants erred, the King was punished. Grace is free only because the giver himself has borne the cost.

"YES," SAID JESUS, "WHAT SORROW ALSO AWAITS YOU EXPERTS IN RELIGIOUS LAW! FOR YOU CRUSH PEOPLE WITH UNBEARABLE RELIGIOUS DEMANDS." OVER TIME, THE SPIRIT OF LAW-KEEPING STIFFENS INTO EXTREMISM. THE SCRIBES AND PHARISEES WHO STUDIED MOSES' LAW, FOR EXAMPLE, TACKED ON MANY ADDITIONS TO ITS 613 REGULATIONS. THE RABBI ELIEZER THE GREAT SPECI-FIED HOW OFTEN A COMMON LABORER SHOULD HAVE SEX WITH HIS WIFE. PHARISEES ADDED SCORES OF EMENDA-TIONS ON SABBATH BEHAV-IOR ALONE. A WOMAN COULD NOT LOOK IN THE MIRROR ON THE SABBATH LEST SHE SEE A GRAY HAIR AND BE TEMPTED TO PLUCK IT OUT.

YOU COULD SWALLOW VINEGAR BUT NOT GARGLE IT. WHATEVER MOSES HAD SAID THE PHARISEES COULD IMPROVE ON. THE THIRD COMMANDMENT, "YOU SHALL NOT MISUSE THE NAME OF THE LORD," BECAME A BAN AGAINST USING THE LORD'S NAME AT ALL, AND THUS TO THIS DAY DEVOUT JEWS WRITE "G–D" INSTEAD OF "GOD" AND NEVER SPEAK THE WORD. "YOU SHALL NOT COMMIT ADULTERY" LED TO PHARISEES' RULES AGAINST TALKING TO OR EVEN LOOKING AT WOMEN WHO WERE NOT THEIR WIVES. "BLEEDING PHARISEES," WHO HAD LOWERED THEIR HEADS AND BUMPED INTO WALLS, WORE THEIR BRUISES AS BADGES OF HOLINESS.

CHAPTER 1.

1 *The creation* of heaven and earth, 3 of the light,
6 of the firmament, 9 of the earth separated from
the waters, 11 and made fruitful, 14 of the sun,
moon, and stars, 20 of fish and fowl, 24 of beasts
and cattle, 26 of man in the image of God. 29
Also the appointment of food.

B. C. 4004.

IN the [a]beginning Daddy created the heaven and the earth.

2 And the earth was without form, and void ; and darkness *was* upon the face of the deep. [c] And the Spirit of Daddy moved upon the face of the waters.

3 [d] And Daddy said, Let there be light : and there was light.

4 And Daddy saw the light, that *it was* good : and Daddy divided [2] the light from the darkness.

a John 1. 1, 2.
Heb. 1. 10.
b Ps. 8. 3 ; 33.
6 ; 89. 11, 12
102. 25 ; 136.
5 ; 146. 6.
Is. 44. 24.
Jer. 10. 12 ;
51. 15.
Zech. 12. 1.
Acts 14. 15 ;
17. 24.
Col. 1. 16, 17
Heb. 11. 3.
Rev. 4. 11.
c Ps. 33. 6.
Is. 40. 13, 14
d Ps. 33. 9.
e 2 Cor. 4. 6.
2 Heb. *between the
light and be
tween the
darkness.*
f Ps. 74. 16 ;
104. 20.
3 Heb. *And*

100

•

3 And the eve
g were the th
4 ¶ And Dadd
lights in the
aven to divid
ght; and let them be for signs,
ad ^{o} for seasons, and for days, and
ears:
5 And let them be for lights in
he firmament of the heaven to give
ght upon the earth: and it was so.
16 And Daddy^p made two great
ghts; the greater light ^{7} to rule
he day, and ^{q} the lesser light to rule
he night: *he made* ^{r} the stars also.
17 And Daddy set them in the fir-
nament of the heaven to give light

During John F. Kennedy's administration, photographers sometimes captured a winsome scene. Seated around the President's desk in gray suits, cabinet members are debating matters of world consequence, such as the Cuban missile crisis. Meanwhile, a toddler, the two-year-old John-John, crawls atop the huge Presidential desk, oblivious to White House protocol and the weighty matters of state. John-John was simply visiting his daddy, and sometimes to his father's delight he would wander into the Oval Office without a knock.————That is the kind of shocking accessibility conveyed in Jesus' word *Abba* (Daddy). God may be the Sovereign Lord of the Universe, but through his Son, God has made himself as approachable as any doting human father.

SOUTH KOREA. Umsong. A Christian volunteer feeds a handicapped child in the "Flower Village" run by Catholic priests.

"TO LOVE A PERSON means to see them as God intended them to be." ---FYODOR DOSTOEVSKY

Not long ago I heard from a pastor friend who was battling with his fifteen-year-old daughter. He knew she was using birth control, and several nights she had not bothered to come home at all. The parents had tried various forms of punishment, to no avail. The daughter lied to them, deceived them, and found a way to turn the tables on them: "It's your fault for being so strict!"

My friend told me, "I remember standing before the plate-glass window in my living room, staring out into the darkness, waiting for her to come home. I felt such rage. I wanted to be like the father of the Prodigal Son, yet I was furious with my daughter for the way she would manipulate us and twist the knife to hurt us. And of course, she was hurting herself more than anyone. I understood then the passages in the prophets expressing God's anger. The people knew how to wound him, and God cried out in pain.

"And I must tell you, when my daughter came home that night, or rather the next morning, I wanted nothing in the world so much as to take her in my arms, to love her, to tell her I wanted the best for her. I was a helpless, lovesick father."

Now, when I think about God, I hold up that image of the lovesick father, which is miles away from the stern monarch I used to envision. I think of my friend standing in front of the plate-glass window gazing achingly into the darkness. I think of Jesus' depiction of the Waiting Father, heartsick, abused, yet wanting above all else to forgive and begin anew, to announce with joy, "This my son was dead, and is alive again; he was lost, and is found."

England

Holland

When someone asked theologian Karl Barth what he would

say to Adolf Hitler, he replied,

"Jesus Christ died for your sins."

Hitler's sins? Has grace no limit?

Switze

East
Prussia

Poland

Austria

d

107

The world

grace.

thirsts for

you, but even as I said these words my heart remained angry or resentful. I still wanted to hear the story that tells me that I was right after all; I still wanted to hear apologies and excuses; I still wanted the satisfaction of receiving some praise in return—if only the praise for being so forgiving!

But God's forgiveness is unconditional; it comes from a heart that does not demand anything for itself, a heart that is completely empty of self-seeking. It is this divine forgiveness that I have to practice in my daily life. It calls me to keep stepping over all my arguments that say forgiveness is unwise, unhealthy, and impractical. It challenges me to step over all my needs for gratitude and compliments. Finally, it demands of me that I step over that wounded part of my heart that feels hurt and wronged and that wants to stay in control and put a few conditions between me and the one whom I am asked to forgive.—*Henri Nouwen*

KU KLUX KLAN GRAND DRAGON LARRY TRAPP of Lincoln, Nebraska, made national headlines in 1992 when he renounced his **HATRED**, tore down his **NAZI** flags, and destroyed his many cartons of **HATE** literature. As Kathryn Watterson recounts in the book Not by the Sword, Trapp had been won over by the forgiving love of a Jewish cantor and his family. Though Trapp had sent them vile pamphlets **MOCKING** big-nosed Jews and denying the Holocaust, though he had **THREATENED** violence in phone calls made to their home, though he had targeted their synagogue for **BOMBING**, the cantor's family consistently responded with compassion and concern. Diabetic since childhood, Trapp was confined to a wheelchair and rapidly going blind; the cantor's family invited Trapp into their home to care for him. "They showed me such love that I couldn't help but love them back," Trapp later said. He spent his last months of life seeking forgiveness from Jewish groups, the NAACP, and the many individuals he had **HATE**d.

JUSTICE HAS A GOOD AND RIGHTEOUS AND RATIONAL KIND OF POWER. THE POWER OF GRACE IS DIFFERENT: UNWORLDLY, TRANSFORMING, SUPERNATURAL. Reginald Denny, the truck driver **ASSAULTED** during the riots in South Central Los Angeles, demonstrated this power of grace. The entire nation watched the helicopter video of two men **SMASHING** his truck window with a brick, **HAULING** him from the cab, then **BEATING** him with a broken bottle and **KICKING** him until the side of his face caved in. In court, his

TORMENTORS were
BELLIGERENT and
UNREPENTANT, yielding no ground. With worldwide media looking on, Reginald Denny, his face still swollen and misshapen, shook off the protests of his lawyers, made his way over to the mothers of the two defendants, hugged them, and told them he forgave them. The mothers embraced Denny, one declaring,

"I love you."

I DO NOT KNOW WHAT EFFECT THAT SCENE HAD ON THE

SURLY DEFENDANTS, SITTING IN HANDCUFFS NOT FAR AWAY.

BUT I DO KNOW THAT FORGIVENESS, AND ONLY

FORGIVENESS, CAN BEGIN TO THAW THE **GUILTY** PARTY.
And I also know what effect it has on me when a fellow
worker, or my wife, comes to me without prompting and offers
forgiveness for some wrong I am too **PROUD** and
STUBBORN to confess.

Forgiveness—undeserved, unearned—can cut the cords and let the oppressive
burden of guilt roll away. The New Testament shows a resurrected Jesus
leading Peter by the hand through a three-fold ritual of forgiveness. Peter
need not go through life with the **GUILTY**, hangdog look of one who has
BETRAYED the Son of God. Oh, no. On the backs of such transformed

> **SINNERS** Christ would build
> his church.

I KNOW HOW EASY IT IS TO GET SWEPT AWAY BY THE POLITICS OF POLARIZATION, TO SHOUT ACROSS PICKET LINES AT THE "ENEMY" ON THE OTHER SIDE. BUT JESUS COMMANDED, "LOVE YOUR ENEMIES." WHO IS MY ENEMY? THE ABORTIONIST? THE HOLLYWOOD PRODUCER POLLUTING OUR CULTURE? THE POLITICIAN THREATENING MY MORAL PRINCIPALS? THE DRUG LORD RULING MY INNER CITY? IF MY ACTIVISM, HOWEVER WELL-MOTIVATED, DRIVES OUT LOVE, THEN I HAVE MISUNDERSTOOD JESUS' GOSPEL. I AM STUCK WITH LAW, NOT THE GOSPEL OF GRACE.

THE ISSUES FACING SOCIETY ARE PIVOTAL, AND PERHAPS A CULTURE WAR IS INEVITABLE. BUT CHRISTIANS SHOULD USE DIFFERENT WEAPONS IN FIGHTING WARS, THE "WEAPONS OF MERCY" IN DOR DAY'S WONDERFUL PHRASE. JESUS DECLARED THY THAT WE SHOULD HAVE ONE DISTINGUISHING MARK: NOT POLITICAL CORRECTNESS OR MORAL SUPERIORITY, PAUL ADDED THAT WITHOUT LOVE NOTHING WE DO—NO MIRACLE OF FAITH, NO THEOLOGICAL BRILLIANCE, NO FLAMING PERSONAL SACRIFICE—WILL AVAIL (1 CORINTHIANS 13).

BUT LOVE

114

TAKING GOD'S ASSIGNMENT SERIOUSLY
MEANS THAT I MUST LEARN TO LOOK AT THE
WORLD UPSIDE DOWN. AS JESUS DID
INSTEAD OF SEEKING OUT PEOPLE WHO
STROKE MY EGO. I FIND THOSE WHOSE
EGOS NEED STROKING
INSTEAD OF IMPORTANT PEOPLE WITH
RESOURCES WHO CAN DO ME FAVORS
I FIND PEOPLE WITH FEW RESOURCES
INSTEAD OF THE STRONG. I LOOK
FOR THE WEAK
INSTEAD OF THE HEALTHY, THE SICK
IS NOT THIS HOW GOD RECONCILES THE
WORLD TO HIMSELF?
DID JESUS NOT INSIST THAT HE
CAME FOR THE SINNERS AND NOT THE
RIGHTEOUS, FOR THE SICK
AND NOT THE HEALTHY?

But here is how God has shown
his love for us.
While we were still sinners,
Christ died for us.
—ROMANS 5:8

115

Our wounds and defects are the very fissures through which grace might pass. It is our human destiny on earth to be imperfect, incomplete, weak, and mortal, and only by accepting that destiny can we escape the force of gravity and receive grace. Only then can we grow close to God.

Although claiming my true identity as a child of God, I still live as though the God to whom I am returning demands an explanation. I still think about his love as conditional and about home as a place I am not yet fully sure of. While walking home, I keep entertaining doubts about whether I will be truly welcome when I get there. As I look at my spiritual journey, my long and fatiguing trip home, I see how full it is of guilt about the past and worries about the future. I realize my failures and know that I lost the dignity of my sonship, but I am not yet able to fully believe that where my failings are great, "grace is always greater." Still clinging to my sense of worthlessness, I project for myself a place far below that which belongs to the son. Belief in total, absolute forgiveness does not come readily.

—HENRI NOUWEN, *The Return of the Prodigal Son*

When you start mathematics you do not begin with calculus; you begin with simple addition. In the same way, if we really want (but all depends on really wanting) to learn to forgive, perhaps we had better start with something easier than the Gestapo. One might start with forgiving one's husband or wife, or parents or children, for something they have done or said in the last week. That will probably keep us busy for the moment.

—CS LEWIS

Frank Reed, an American citizen held hostage in Lebanon, disclosed upon his release that he had not spoken to one of his fellow hostages for several months following some minor dispute. Most of that time, the two feuding hostages hadbeenchainedtogether.

Jesus reduced the mark of a Christian to one word. "By this all men will know that you are my disciples," he said: "if you love one another." The most subversive act the church can take is consistently to obey that one command.

Think of the impact if the first thing radical feminists thought of when the conversation turned to evangelical men was that they had the best reputation for keeping their marriage vows and serving their wives in the costly fashion of Jesus at the cross. Think of the impact if the first thing the homosexual community thought of when someone mentioned evangelicals was that they were the people who lovingly ran the AIDS shelters and tenderly cared for them down to the last gasp. A little consistent wholesome modeling and costly servanthood are worth millions of true words spoken harshly.

When we look through the eyes of Jesus, we see new things in people. In the murderers, we see our own hatred. In the addicts, we see our own addictions. In the saints, we catch glimpses of our own holiness. We can see our own brokenness, our own violence, our own ability to destroy, and we can see our own sacredness, our own capacity to love and forgive. When we realize that we are both wretched and beautiful, we are freed up to see others the same way. —SHANE CLAIBORNE

Repent, then, and turn to God, so that your sins may be wiped out, that times of refreshing may come from the Lord.
—ACTS 3:19

"When he came to his senses, he said, 'How many of my father's hired men have food to spare, and here I am starving to death! I will set out and go back to my father and say to him: Father, I have sinned against heaven and against you. I am no longer worthy to be called your son; make me like one of your hired men.' So he got up and went to his father.

"But while he was still a long way off, his father saw him and was filled with compassion for him; he ran to his son, threw his arms around him and kissed him.

"The son said to him, 'Father, I have sinned against heaven and against you. I am no longer worthy to be called your son.'

"But the father said to his servants, 'Quick! Bring the best robe and put it on him. Put a ring on his finger and sandals on his feet. Bring the fattened calf and kill it. Let's have a feast and celebrate. For this son of mine was dead and is alive again; he was lost and is found.' "
—JESUS, LUKE 15:17-24

Being unwanted, unloved, uncared for, forgotten
by everybody, I think that is a much greater hunger,
a much greater poverty than the person who has
nothing to eat. —MOTHER TERESA

The Gospels tell the story of a group of people who are ready to stone
an adulteress. (Stoning was the legal consequence of adultery.) They
ask Jesus for his support of this death-penalty case. His response is that
they are all adulterers. He says, :Let any one of you who is without sin
be the first to throw a stone at her." (John 8:7) And the people drop
their stones and walk away with their heads bowed. We want to kill the
murderers, but Jesus says that we are all murderers: "Anyone who is
angry with a brother or a sister will be subject to judgement. Again,
anyone who says to a brother or sister, 'Raca' is answerable to the
Sanhedrin. And anyone who says, 'You fool!' will be in danger of
the fire of hell" (Matt. 5:22). Again the stones drop. We are all
murderers and adulterers and terrorists. And we are all precious.
—SHANE CLAIBORNE

God wants something more intimate than
the closest relationship on earth, the
lifetime bond between a man and a woman.
What God wants is not a good performance,
but my heart.

EARLY ON, STALIN BUILT a village in Poland called Nowa Huta, or "New Town," to demonstrate the promise of communism. He could not change the entire country at once, he said, but he could construct one new town with a shiny steel factory, spacious apartments, plentiful parks, and broad streets as a token of what would follow.

What if Christians used that same approach in secular society and succeeded? "In the world the Christians are a colony of the true home," said Bonhoeffer. Perhaps Christians should work harder towards establishing colonies that point to our true home. All too often the church holds up a mirror reflecting back the society around it, rather than a window revealing a different way.

If the world despises a notorious sinner, the church will love her.

If the world cuts off aid to the poor and suffering, the church will offer food and healing.

If the world oppresses, the church will raise up the oppressed.

If the world shames a social outcast, the church will proclaim God's reconciling love.

If the world seeks profit and self-fulfillment, the church seeks sacrifice and service.

If the world demands retribution, the church dispenses grace.

If the world splinters into factions, the church joins together in unity.

If the world destroys its enemies, the church loves them.

That, at least, is the vision of the church in the New Testament:
a colony of heaven in a hostile world.

like me.

like me.

Martin Luther King had developed a sophisticated strategy of war fought with grace, not gunpowder. He never refused to meet with his adversaries. He opposed policies but not personalities. Most importantly, he countered violence with nonviolence, and hatred with love. "Let us not seek to satisfy our thirst for freedom by drinking from the cup of bitterness and hatred," he exhorted his followers. "We must not allow our creative protest to degenerate into physical violence. Again and again, we must rise to the majestic heights of meeting physical force with soul force." King's associate Andrew Young remembers those turbulent days as a time when they sought to save "black men's bodies and white men's souls." Their real goal, King said, was not to defeat the white man but "to awaken a sense of shame within the oppressor and challenge his false sense of superiority...The end is reconciliation; the end is redemption; the end is the creation of the beloved community."

Robert Fahsenfeldt, owner of a segregated lunchroom in the racially tense community of Cambridge, Md., douses a white integrationist with water, July 8, 1963. The integrationist, Edward Dickerson, was among three white and eight Negro protesters who knelt on the sidewalk in front of the restaurant to sing freedom songs. A raw egg, which Fahsenfeldt had broken over Dickerson's head moments earlier, still is visible on the back of Dickerson's head. *(AP Photo/stf)*

I marvel at Jesus'
tenderness in dealing with people.

John gives
the account of Jesus'
impromptu

conversation with a woman at a well.

In those days the husband initiated the
divorce: this Samaritan woman had been dumped

by five different men.

Jesus could have begun by pointing out
what a mess the woman had made of her life.

Yet he did not say, "Young woman, do you realize what an immoral thing you're

doing, living with a man who

is not your husband?"

Rather he said, in effect,

I sense you are very thirsty. Jesus went on to tell her that the water she was
drinking would never satisfy and then offered her living

water to quench her thirst forever.

I try to recall this spirit of Jesus when I encounter someone of whom I morally
disapprove. This must

be a very

thirsty person,
I tell myself I once
talked with
the priest Henri Nouwen just after he
had returned from San Francisco. He had visited various ministries to
AIDS victims and
was moved with compassion by their sad stories.
"They want love so bad, it's
literally killing them," he said. He saw them as thirsty people
panting after
t h e wrong kind
of water.

When I am tempted to recoil in horror
from sinners, from
"different" people, I remember what it must have been like for
Jesus to live on earth. Perfect, sinless, Jesus
had every right to be repulsed by the
behavior of
those around him.
Yet he treated notorious
sinners with mercy and
not
judgment.

If I had to summarize the primary New Testament motivation for "being good" in one word, I would choose gratitude. Paul begins most of his letters with a summary of the riches we possess in Christ. If we comprehend what Christ has done for us, then surely out of gratitude we will strive to live "worthy" of such great love. We will strive for holiness not to make God love us but because he already does. As Paul told Titus, it is the grace of God that "teaches us to say 'No' to ungodliness and worldly passions, and to live self-controlled, upright and godly lives."

In her memoir *Ordinary Time*, the Catholic writer Nancy Mairs tells of her years of mutiny against childhood images of a "Daddy God," who could only be pleased if she followed a list of onerous prescriptions and prohibitions:

The fact that these took their **most basic form as commandments** suggested that human nature had to be forced into goodness; left to its own devices, it would prefer idols, **profanity, leisurely Sunday mornings** with bagels and the New York Times, disrespect for authority, murder, adultery, theft, lies, and everything belonging to the guy next door.... I was forever on the perilous verge of doing a don't, to atone for which I had to beg forgiveness from the very being who had set me up for trespass, by forbidding behaviors he clearly expected me to commit, in the first place: the God of the Gotcha, you might say.

Mairs broke a lot of those rules, felt constantly guilty, and then, in her words, "learned to thrive in the care of" a God who "asks for the single act that will make transgression impossible: love."

The best reason to be good is to want to be good. Internal change requires relationship. It requires love. "Who can be good, if not made so by loving?" asked Augustine. When Augustine made the famous statement, "If you but love God you may do as you incline," he was perfectly serious. A person who truly loves God will be inclined to please God, which is why Jesus and Paul both summed up the entire law in the simple command, "Love God."

If we truly grasped the wonder of God's love for us, the devious question that prompted Romans 6 and 7—What can I get away with?— would never even occur to us. We would spend our days trying to fathom

God's grace.

+++++IN 1987 AN IRA BOMB WENT OFF in a small town west of Belfast, amid a group of Protestants who had gathered to honor the war dead on Veteran's Day. Eleven people died and sixty-three others were wounded. What made this act of terrorism stand out from so many others was the response of one of the wounded, Gordon Wilson, a devout Methodist who had emigrated north from the Irish Republic to work as a draper. The bomb buried Wilson and his twenty-year-old daughter under five feet of concrete and brick. "Daddy, I love you very much," were the last words Marie spoke, grasping her father's hand as they waited for the rescuers. She suffered severe spinal and brain injuries, and died a few hours later in the hospital.— — — — — — — — — —

+++A newspaper proclaimed, "No one remembers what the politicians had to say at that time. No one who heard Gordon Wilson will ever forget what he confessed ... His grace towered over the miserable justifications of the bombers." Speaking from his hospital bed, WILSON SAID, *"I have lost my daughter,*

BUT

I bear no grudge. Bitter talk is not going to bring Marie Wilson back to life. I shall pray, tonight and every night, that God will forgive them."

+++His daughter's last words were words of love, and Gordon Wilson determined to live out his life on that plane of love. "The world wept," said one report, as Wilson gave a similar interview over BBC radio that week.

+ + + After his release from the hospital, Gordon Wilson led a crusade for Protestant-Catholic reconciliation. Protestant extremists who had planned to avenge the bombing decided, because of the publicity surrounding Wilson, that such behavior would be politically foolish. Wilson wrote a book about his daughter, spoke against violence, and constantly repeated the refrain, "Love is the bottom line." He met with the IRA, personally forgave them for what they had done, and asked them to lay down their arms. "I know that you've lost loved ones, just like me," he told them. "Surely, enough is enough. Enough blood has been spilled." —

+ + + The Irish Republic ultimately made Wilson a member of its Senate. When he died in 1995, the Irish Republic, Northern Ireland, and all of Great Britain honored this ordinary Christian citizen who had gained fame for his uncommon spirit of grace and forgiveness. His spirit exposed by contrast the violent deeds of retaliation, and his life of peacemaking came to symbolize the craving for peace within many others who would never make the headlines. —

+ + + "To bless the people who have oppressed our spirits, emotionally deprived us, or in other ways handicapped us, is the most extraordinary work any of us will ever do," [Elizabeth O'Connor] . — — — — — — —

JAPAN. Tokyo. In debt and under threat, Hiroyuki Suzuki abandoned life as a Yakuza gangster for the brotherhood of Christ. Suzuki putting on his robe. His Yakuza tattoos show his former life.

SEPTEMBER 1999

26 27 28 29

182

When Jesus loved a guilt-laden person and helped him, he saw in him an erring child of God. He saw in him a human being whom his Father loved and grieved over because he was going wrong. He saw him as God originally designed and meant him to be, and therefore he saw through the SURFACE LAYER of grime and dirt to the real man underneath. —HELMUT THIELICKE

I know why some christians act so ungraciously: out of **fear.**

categories as crime, divorce

the united

outranks every other industrialized country.

social conservatives feel more and

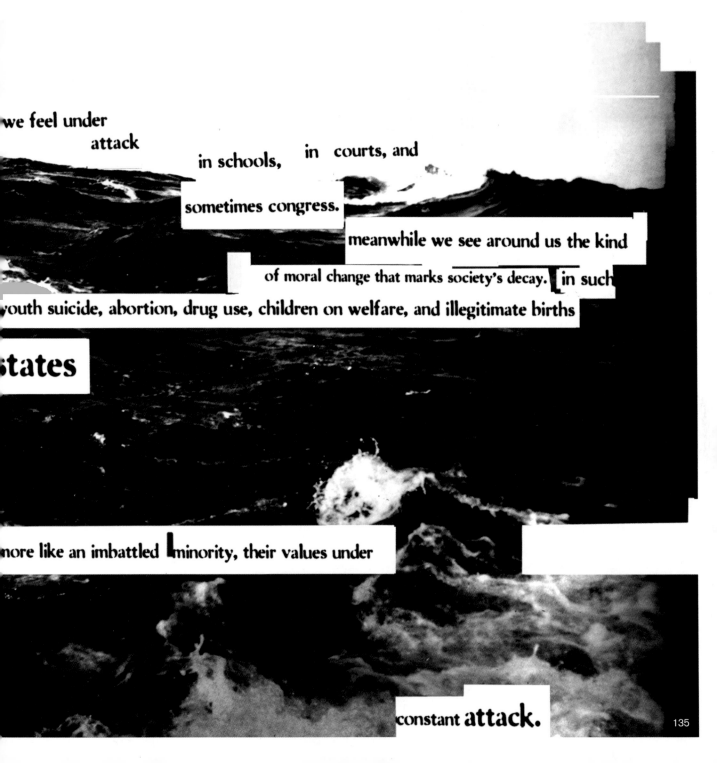

we feel under
attack
in schools, in courts, and
sometimes congress.

meanwhile we see around us the kind
of moral change that marks society's decay. in such
youth suicide, abortion, drug use, children on welfare, and illegitimate births

states

more like an imbattled minority, their values under

constant **attack.**

135

In a scene from the movie *Ironweed,* the characters played by Jack Nicholson and Meryl Streep stumble across an old Eskimo woman lying in the snow, probably drunk. Besotted themselves, the two debate what they should do about her.

"IS SHE DRUNK OR A BUM?" ASKS NICHOLSON.

"JUST A BUM. BEEN ONE ALL HER LIFE."

"AND BEFORE THAT?"

"SHE WAS A WHORE IN ALASKA."

"SHE HASN'T BEEN A WHORE ALL HER LIFE. BEFORE THAT?"

"I DUNNO. JUST A LITTLE KID, I GUESS."

"WELL A LITTLE KID'S SOMETHING. IT'S NOT A BUM AND IT'S NOT A WHORE. IT'S SOMETHING. LET'S TAKE HER IN."

The two vagrants were seeing the Eskimo woman through the lens of grace. Where society saw only a bum and a whore, grace saw "a little kid," a person made in the image of God no matter how defaced that image had become.

136

The
Cold War, says   former
Senator Sam Nunn,
ended "not in a nuclear inferno, but in a blaze
of candles in the churches of Eastern Europe." Candlelight processions in East
Germany did not show up well on the evening news, but they helped change the face of
the globe. First a few hundred, then a thousand, then   thirty   thousand,
fifty thousand, and finally five hundred thousand—nearly the entire population of the city—turned out in
Leipzig for candlelight vigils. After a prayer meeting at St. Nikolai Church, the peaceful protestors
would   march
through the dark streets, singing hymns.   Police
and soldiers with all their weapons seemed powerless against
such a force. Ultimately, on the night a similar march in East Berlin attracted one
million protestors, the hated Berlin Wall
came tumbling down without a shot being fired.   A   huge
banner appeared across a Leipzig   street:
Wir Danken
Dir, Kirche (We   thank   you,
church).

PART FOUR →

THAT WAS NOT Jesus' point,
Margaret. All three stories emphasize the
finder's joy. True, the prodigal returned home
of his own free will, but clearly the central focus of
the story is the father's outrageous love: "But while he
was still a long way off, his father saw him and was filled
with compassion for him; he ran to his son, threw his arms
around him and kissed him." When the son tries to repent,
the father interrupts his prepared speech in order to get the
celebration under way. → A missionary in Lebanon once
read this parable to a group of villagers who lived in a
culture very similar to the one Jesus described and
who had never heard the story. "What do you
notice?" he asked. Two details of the
story stood out to the villagers.
First, by claiming

his inheritance early, the son was saying to his father, "I wish you were dead!" The villagers could not imagine a patriarch taking such an insult or agreeing to the son's demand. ⇗ Second, they noticed that the father ran to greet his long-lost son. In the Middle East, a man of stature walks with slow and stately dignity; never does he run. In Jesus' story the father runs, and Jesus' audience no doubt gasped at this detail. ⇗ Grace is unfair, which is one of the hardest things about it. It is unreasonable to expect a woman to forgive the terrible things her father did to her just because he apologizes many years later, and totally unfair to ask that a mother overlook the many offenses her teenage son committed. Grace, however, is not about fairness. ⇗ What is true of families is also true of tribes, races, and nations.

God loves us
because
of who He is
and not
because of
who
we are.

Rebecca is a quiet woman.

She married a pastor who had some renown as a retreat leader. It became apparent, however, that her husband had a dark side. He dabbled in pornography, and on his trips to other cities he solicited prostitutes. Sometimes he asked Rebecca for **forgive**ness, sometimes he did not. In time, he left her for another woman, Julianne.

Rebecca told us how painful it was for her, a pastor's wife, to suffer this humiliation. Some church members who had respected her husband treated her as if his sexual straying had been her fault. Devastated, she found herself PULLING AWAY FROM HUMAN CONTACT, UNABLE TO TRUST ANOTHER PERSON. SHE COULD NEVER PUT HER HUSBAND OUT OF MIND BECAUSE THEY HAD CHILDREN AND SHE HAD TO MAKE REGULAR CONTACT WITH HIM IN ORDER TO ARRANGE HIS VISITATION PRIVILEGES.

REBECCA HAD THE INCREASING SENSE THAT UNLESS SHE **FORGAVE** HER FORMER HUSBAND, A HARD LUMP OF REVENGE WOULD BE PASSED ON TO THEIR CHILDREN. FOR MONTHS SHE PRAYED. AT FIRST HER PRAYERS SEEMED AS VENGEFUL AS SOME OF THE PSALMS: SHE ASKED GOD TO GIVE HER EX-HUSBAND "WHAT HE DESERVED." FINALLY SHE CAME TO THE PLACE OF LETTING GOD, NOT HERSELF, DETERMINE "WHAT HE DESERVED."

One night Rebecca called her ex-husband and said, in a shaky, strained voice, "I want you to know that I **forgive** you for what you've done to me. And I **forgive** Julianne too." He laughed off her apology, unwilling to admit he had done anything wrong. Despite his rebuff, that conversation helped Rebecca get past her bitter feelings.

A few years later Rebecca got a hysterical phone call from Julianne, the woman who had "stolen" her husband.

She had been attending a   ministerial conference with him
in Minneapolis, and he had left the
hotel room to go for a walk.

A few hours passed, then
Julianne heard from the police: her
husband had been picked up for
soliciting a prostitute.

On the phone with Rebecca, Julianne was sobbing.
"I never believed you," she said. "I kept telling myself that
even if what you said was true, he had changed.

And now this. I feel so ashamed, and hurt, and guilty.
I have no one on earth who can understand.

Then I remembered the night when you said you **forgave** us. I
thought maybe you could understand what I'm going through. It's a
terrible thing to ask, I know, but
could I come talk to you?"

Somehow Rebecca found the courage to invite Julianne
over that same evening. They sat in her living room,
cried together, shared stories of betrayal, and in
the end prayed together. Julianne now points to that
night as the time when she became a Christian.

"For a long time, I had felt foolish about **forgiving** my
husband," Rebecca told us. "But that night I realized
the fruit of **forgive**ness. Julianne was right. I could
understand what she was going through. And because I
had been there too, I could be on her side, instead of
her enemy. We both had been betrayed by the same man.
Now it was up to me to teach her how to overcome the
hatred and revenge and guilt she was feeling."

From the Gospels' accounts, it seems **forgive**ness was not easy for God,
either. "My Father, if it is possible, take this cup away from me,"
Jesus prayed, contemplating the cost, and the sweat rolled off him
like drops of blood. There was no other way. Finally, in one of his
last statements before dying, he said, "**Forgive** them"—all of them,
the Roman soldiers, the religious leaders, his disciples who had fled
in darkness, you, me—

"**Forgive** them, Father! They don't know what they
are doing." Only by becoming a human being could
the Son of God truly say, "They don't know what
they are doing." Having lived among us, he now
understood.

THERE IS A SIMPLE CURE FOR PEOPLE who doubt God's love and question God's grace: to turn to the Bible and examine the kind of people God loves. Jacob, who *dared take God on in a wrestling match* and ever after bore a wound from that struggle, became the eponym for God's people, the "children of Israel." The Bible tells of a *murderer* and *adulterer* who gained a reputation as the greatest king of the Old Testament, a *"man after God's own heart."* And of a church being led by a disciple who *cursed and swore that he had never known Jesus.* And of a missionary being recruited from the ranks of the *Christian-torturers.* I get mailings from Amnesty International, and as I look at their photos of men and women who have been *beaten* and *cattle-prodded* and *jabbed* and *spit on* and *electrocuted,* I ask myself, "What kind of human being could do that to another human being?" Then I read the book of Acts and meet the kind of person who could do such a thing (Paul)—now an apostle of grace, a servant of Jesus Christ, the greatest missionary history has ever known. If God can love *that kind of person*, maybe, just maybe, he can love the likes of me. ✪✪✪✪

BELOW: Miriam Ngaujah, 5, smiles as she sits on the lap of her uncle Aiah Kassingbma, whose functionless hand was reattached after rebels mutilated him during an advance known as "Operation No Living Thing." Thousands of people lost everything in Sierra Leone's civil war, systematically butchered by a rebel movement with a fascination for amputation and an undefined political agenda.

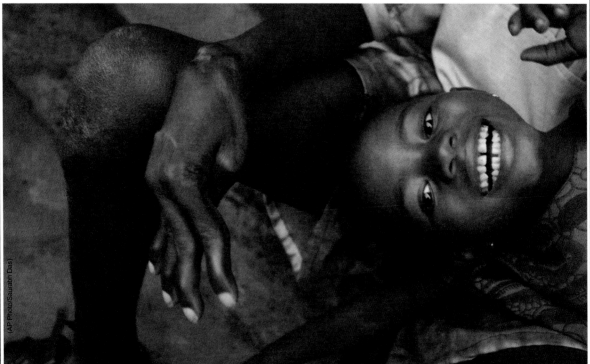

(AP Photo/Saurabh Das)

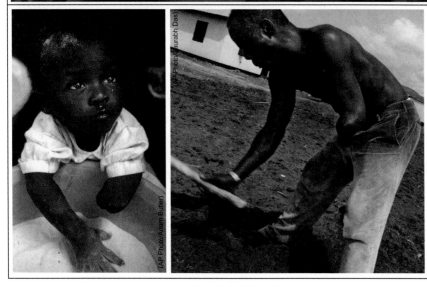

(AP Photo/Adam Butler)

(AP Photo/Saurabh Das)

FAR LEFT: Marie Koroome helps herself to bulgar wheat. Marie's left arm was intentionally lopped off by rebels around Christmas, in the village of Yuduwa, in the Bombali district, northern Sierra Leone.
NEAR LEFT: Edward Conteh hoes a patch of land near his home in Freetown, Sierra Leone, May 18, 2002. Desperate for a chance to rebuild their shattered lives, Sierra Leone's people say they are ready to forgive the rebels who systematically raped women and girls, and hacked off the hands and feet even of babies. "They are our brothers. We should come together," Conteh said, so future generations can live in "peace and harmony."

NELSON MANDELA taught the world a lesson in grace when, after emerging from prison after twenty-seven years and being elected president of South Africa, he asked his jailer to join him on the inauguration platform. He then appointed Archbishop Desmond Tutu to head an official government panel with the daunting name, the Truth and Reconciliation Commission. Mandela sought to defuse the natural pattern of revenge that he had seen in so many countries where one oppressed race or tribe took control from another.

For the next two-and-a-half years, South Africans listened to reports of atrocities coming out of the TRC hearings. The rules were simple: if a white policeman or army officer voluntarily faced his accusers, confessed his crime, and fully acknowledged his guilt, he could not be tried and punished for that crime. Hard-liners grumbled about the obvious injustice of letting criminals go free, but Mandela insisted that the country needed healing even more than it needed justice.

At one TRC hearing a policeman named van de Broek recounted an incident when he and other officers shot an eighteen-year-old boy and burned the body. Eight years later van de Broek returned to the same house and seized the boy's father. The wife was forced to watch as policemen bound her husband on a woodpile, poured gasoline over his body, and ignited it.

The courtroom grew hushed as the elderly woman who had lost first her son and then her husband was given a chance to respond.

"WHAT DO YOU WANT FROM MR. VAN DE BROEK?"
the judge asked.

She said she wanted van de Broek to go to the place where they burned her husband's body and gather up the dust so she could give him a decent burial. His head down, the policeman nodded agreement.

Then she added a further response, "Mr. van de Broek took all my family away from me, and I still have a lot of love to give. Twice each month, I would like for him to come to the ghetto and spend a day with me so I can be a mother to him. And I would like Mr. van de Broek to know that he is forgiven by God, and that I forgive him too. I would like to embrace him so he can know my forgiveness is real."

Spontaneously, some in the courtroom began singing "Amazing Grace" as the elderly woman made her way to the witness stand, but van de Broek did not hear the hymn. He fainted, overwhelmed.

Justice was not done in South Africa that day, nor in the entire country during months of agonizing procedures by the TRC. Something beyond justice took place.

"Do not be overcome by evil, but overcome evil with good," said Paul. Nelson Mandela and Desmond Tutu understood that when evil is done, one response alone can overcome the evil. Revenge perpetuates the evil. Justice punishes it. Evil is overcome by good if the injured party absorbs it, refusing to allow it to go any further. And that is the pattern of otherworldly grace that Jesus showed in his life and death.

PEOPLE ARE PREPARED FOR EVERY-
THING EXCEPT FOR THE FACT THAT
BEYOND THE DARKNESS OF THEIR
BLINDNESS THERE IS A GREAT
LIGHT. THEY ARE PREPARED TO GO
ON BREAKING THEIR BACKS PLOWING
THE SAME OLD FIELD WITHOUT
SEEING, UNTIL THEY STUB THEIR
TOES ON IT, THAT THERE IS A
TREASURE BURIED IN THAT FIELD
RICH ENOUGH TO BUY TEXAS. THEY
ARE PREPARED FOR A GOD WHO

STRIKES HARD BARGAINS BUT NOT FOR A GOD WHO GIVES AS MUCH FOR AN HOUR'S WORK AS FOR A DAYS THEY ARE PREPARED FOR A MUSTARD SEED KINGDOM OF GOD BUT NOT FOR THE GREAT BANYAN IT BECOMES WITH BIRDS IN ITS BRANCHES SINGING MOZART. THEY ARE PREPARED FOR THE POTLUCK SUPPER AT FIRST PRESBYTERIAN BUT NOT FOR THE MARRIAGE SUPPER OF THE LAMB. — FREDERICK BUECHNER

153

We're all BASTARDS but

154

GOD

loves

us

anyway.

(SEE PAGE 45)

155

Grace means that no mistake we make in life disqualifies us from God's love. It means that no person is beyond redemption, no human stain beyond cleansing.

grace

how sweet

sweet the

sweet

grac e

sweet

sweet

the sound—

e

how sweet

like me! the

sound—

-how sweet the sound—

sweet

Grace is irrational, unfair, unjust, and only makes sense if I believe in another world governed by a merciful God who always offers another chance. That saved

MEN

ng grace

That saved a wretch like me!

nd—

grace

ng grace

A-MEN.

how sweet

A-MEN.

sweet

sweet

CREATIVE DEVELOPMENT: **MARK ARNOLD, PETE GALL, KURT WILSON**

Special thanks to Jon Arnold and Rick James for their invaluable feedback throughout the creative process.

cover	PHOTOGRAPHER:	**Adam Nadal**	polarisimages.com
8-11	PHOTOGRAPHER:	**Stock**	youworkforthem.com
12-13	PHOTOGRAPHER:	**Mary Ellen Mark**	maryellenmark.com
14-15	PHOTOGRAPHER:	**Andy Anderson**	andyandersonphoto.com
16-17	PHOTOGRAPHER:	**Michael Eastman** *(bus stop)*	eastmanimages.com
16-17	PHOTOGRAPHER:	**Jodie Allen** *(football)*	freshartphotography.com
19	PHOTOGRAPHER:	**Peter Marlow**	magnumphotos.com
27	PHOTOGRAPHER:	**Chris Steele-Perkins**	magnumphotos.com
36, 37	PHOTOGRAPHER:	**Andy Anderson**	andyandersonphoto.com
38-39	ILLUSTRATION:	**Scorsone Drueding**	info@sdposter.com
42-43	PHOTOGRAPHER:	**Jim Goldberg**	magnumphotos.com
48, 49	PHOTOGRAPHER:	**Andy Anderson**	andyandersonphoto.com
56	PHOTOGRAPHER:	**Jim Goldberg** (+stock)	magnumphotos.com
62	PHOTOGRAPHER:	**Stock**	youworkforthem.com
74	PHOTOGRAPHER:	**Stock**	youworkforthem.com
84-85	PHOTOGRAPHER:	**Alex Webb**	magnumphotos.com
86	PHOTOGRAPHER:	**Andy Anderson**	andyandersonphoto.com
94	PHOTOGRAPHER:	**Paul Moore**	paul@spout.com
102-03	PHOTOGRAPHER:	**Abbas**	magnumphotos.com
107	ILLUSTRATION:	**Hudson Talbott**	hudsontalbott.com
110-11	PHOTOGRAPHER:	**Dirk Rees**	peterbailey.co.uk
122, 123	PHOTOGRAPHER:	**Andy Anderson**	andyandersonphoto.com
124	PHOTOGRAPHER:	**Bob Adelman**	magnumphotos.com
132-33	PHOTOGRAPHER:	**Bruce Gilden**	magnumphotos.com
134-35	PHOTOGRAPHER:	**James Schwartz, Bus-9**	bus9productions.com
136	DESIGNER:	**Jon Arnold**	thecoolville.com
144-45	PHOTOGRAPHER:	**Stock**	youworkforthem.com
146	PHOTOGRAPHER:	**Thomas Dworzak**	magnumphotos.com
147	PHOTOGRAPHER:	**Paolo Pellegrin**	magnumphotos.com
152-53	DESIGNER:	**Jon Arnold**	thecoolville.com
154-55	PHOTOGRAPHER:	**Bruno Barbey**	magnumphotos.com

69, 70, 80-81, 90-91, 125 and 149 from **AP Images** apimages.com

35, 60, 61, 64, 67, 104-05 and 107 from **Getty Images** gettyimages.com

PROJECT DEVELOPMENT: John Topliff, Cort Langeland

List of excerpts from WHAT'S SO AMAZING ABOUT GRACE? by Philip Yancey

visualgracebook.com